All the Best

FOR CHRISTMAS PIANO

A Treasury of Classics Arranged for Solo Piano

20 Arrangements

by

Jolene Boyd, Marilynn Ham, Phillip Keveren, Myra Schubert,

Carolyne Taylor, Emily Tufenkjian, Teresa Wilhelmi

Lillenas PUBLISHING COMPANY

KANSAS CITY, MO 64141

lillenas.com

D1561070

Contents

* These songs can be combined into 2 or 3 song medleys.

Christmas Minuet

Bring a Torch, Jeanette Isabella
In the setting of J. S. Bach's *Minuet*

French Carol
Arranged by Carolyne M. Taylor

6

Angels, from the Realms of Glory

In the setting of J. S. Bach's *Gavotte*
and Pachelbel's *Canon in D*

HENRY T. SMART
Arranged by Emily Tufenkjian

Lively ♩ = ca. 96

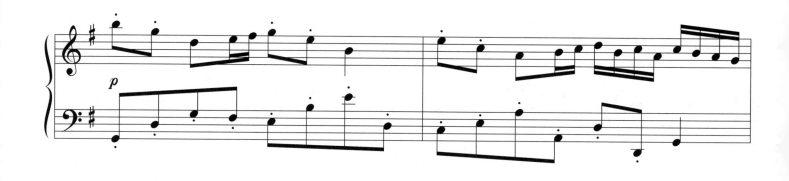

What Child Is This?

Traditional English Melody
Arranged by Jolene Boyd

Flowing ♩ = ca. 84

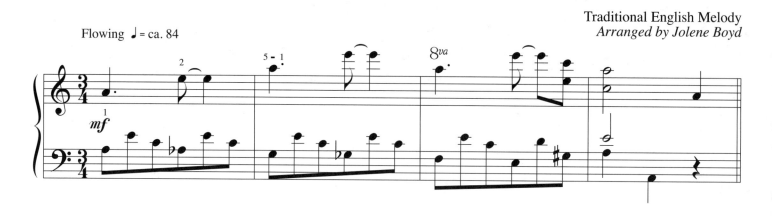

O Holy Night

ADOLPHE C. ADAM
Arranged by Myra Schubert

Flowing ♩. = ca. 66

Christmas Montage

O Come, O Come, Emmanuel
Silent Night! Holy Night!
Angels We Have Heard on High

Arranged by Teresa Wilhelmi

Wistfully ♩ = ca. 60
"O Come, O Come, Emmanuel" (Plainsong)

"Angels We Have Heard on High" (Traditional French Melody)

A Christmas Processional

O Come, All Ye Faithful
Joyful, Joyful, We Adore Thee

Arranged by Marilynn Ham

Stately and majestic ♩ = ca.108

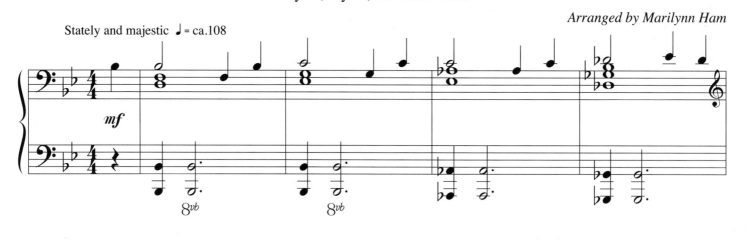

"O Come, All Ye Faithful" (JOHN F. WADE)

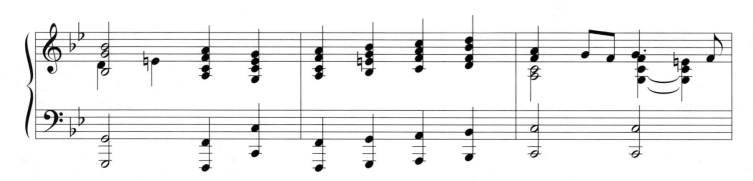

It Came upon the Midnight Clear

RICHARD S. WILLIS
Arranged by Phillip Keveren

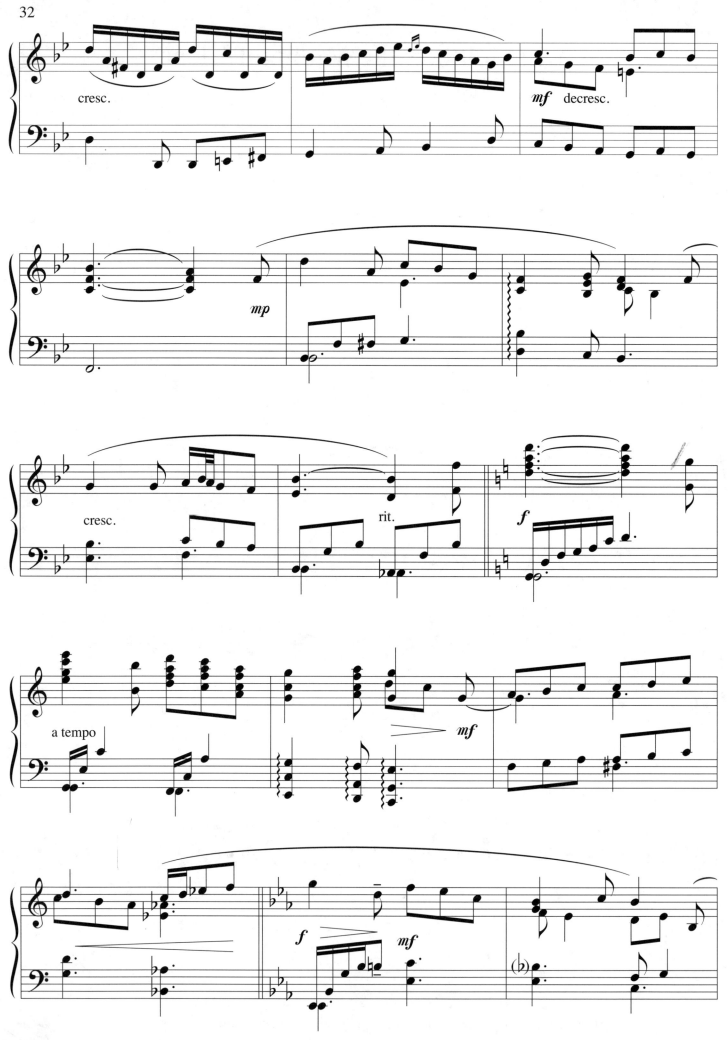

Hark! the Herald Angels Sing

FELIX MENDELSSOHN
Arranged by Phillip Keveren

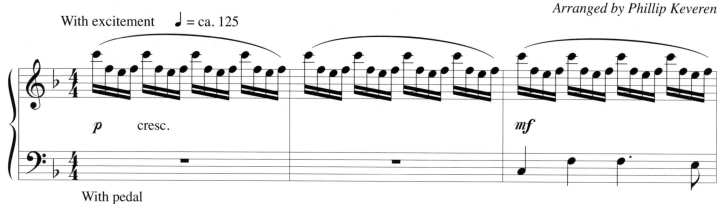

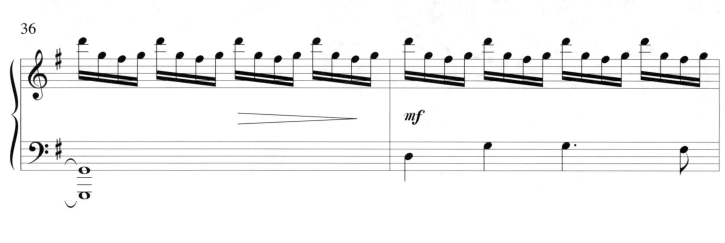

molto rit.

Song ending

Optional transition ending

Simply

sub. *p*

a tempo

Away in a Manger

JAMES R. MURRAY
Arranged by Phillip Keveren

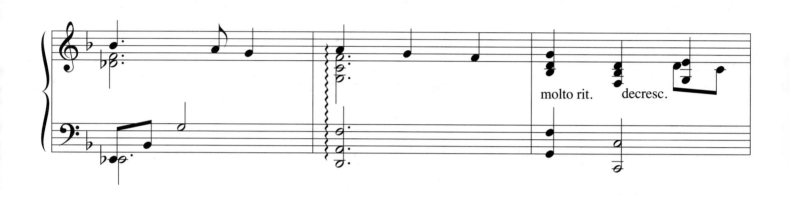

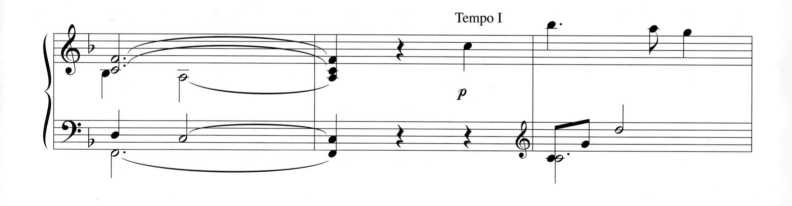

Deck the Halls

In the setting of M. Clementi's *Sonatina, op. 36, no. 3*

Welsh Air
Arranged by Carolyne M. Taylor

44

O Little Town of Bethlehem

LEWIS H. REDNER
Arranged by Jolene Boyd

Expressively ♩ = ca. 88

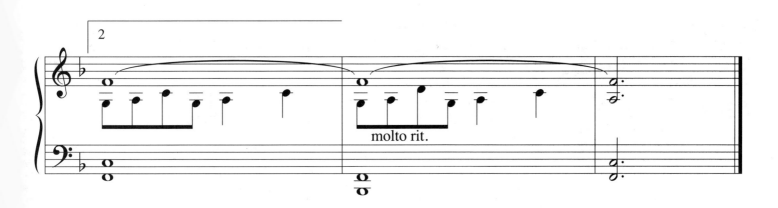

The First Noel

In the setting of J. S. Bach's *Minuet*

W. Sandy's *Christmas Carols*
Arranged by Emily Tufenkjian

Moderato ♩ = ca. 100

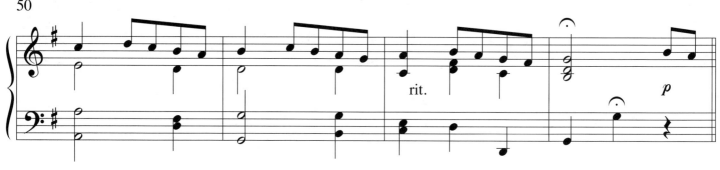

We Three Kings

In the setting of P. I. Tchaikowsky's *Arab Dance*

JOHN HOPKINS
Arranged by Carolyne M. Taylor

Allegro ♩ = ca. 120

dim. e rit.

Thou Didst Leave Thy Throne

TIMOTHY R. MATTHEWS
Arranged by Myra Schubert

Quietly, reverently   ♩ = ca. 60

Go, Tell It on the Mountain

American Folk Song
Arranged by Teresa Wilhelmi

Here We Come A-Caroling

Traditional English Melody
Arranged by Jolene Boyd

Happily ♩ = ca. 132

L.H. detached

Christmas Arabesque

God Rest Ye Merry, Gentlemen
In the setting of Burgmüller's *L'Arabesque*

English Melody
Arranged by Carolyne M. Taylor

Allegro ♩ = ca. 120

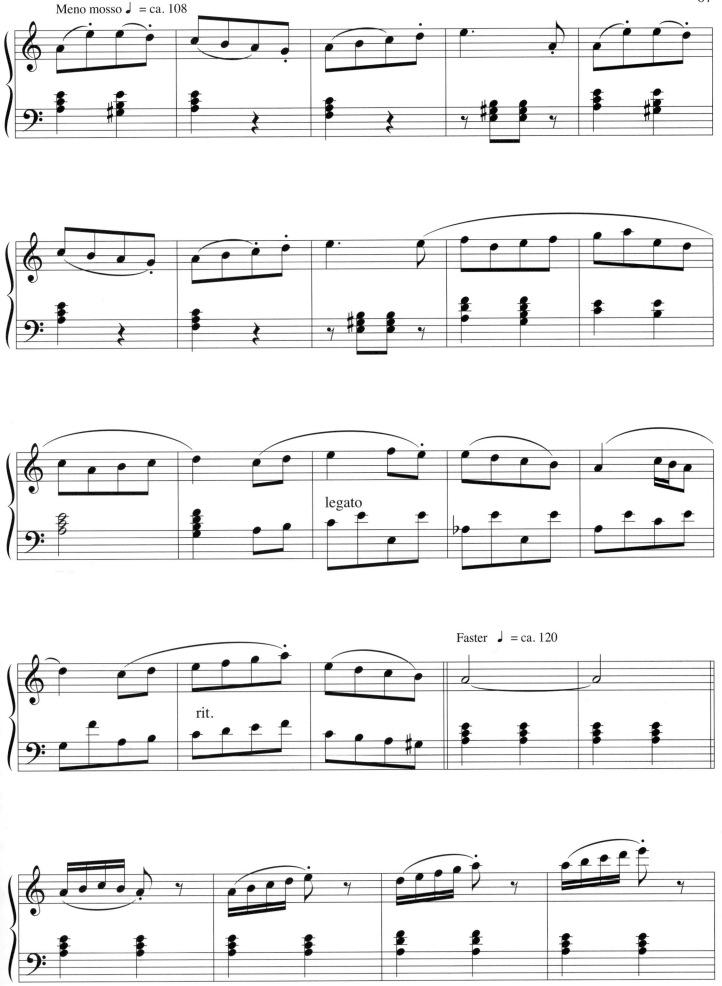

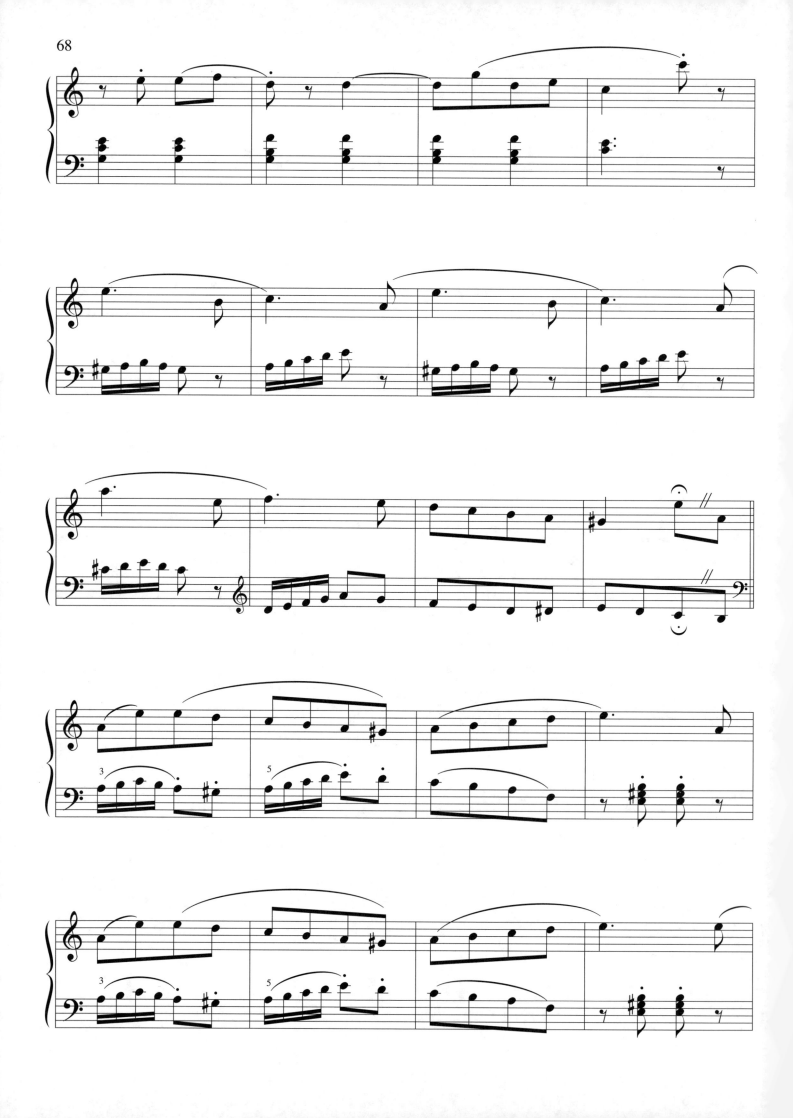

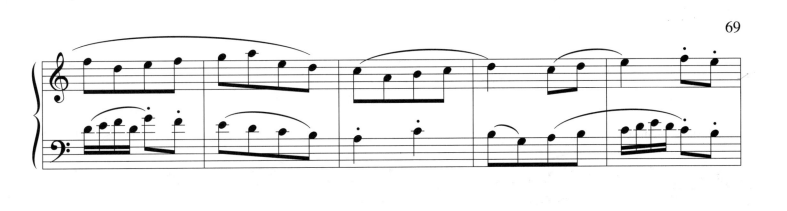

cresc.

dolce

8va - - - - - - - -

March of the Kings

In the setting of J. S. Bach's *Musette*

Traditional French Melody
Arranged by Emily Tufenkjian

Moderate march ♩ = ca. 126

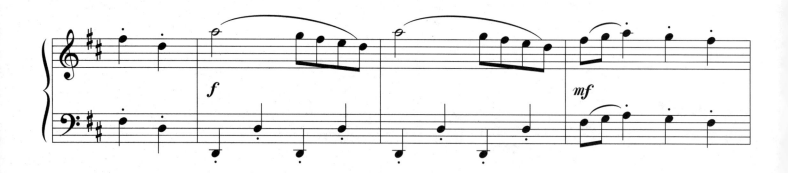

The Angels' Gloria

Gloria
Angels We Have Heard on High

Arranged by Marilynn Ham

Allegro ♩ = ca. 112

"Gloria" (ANTONIO VIVALDI)

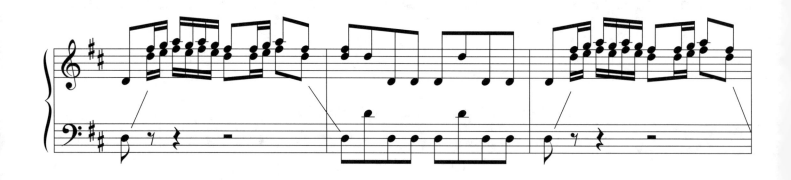

"Angels We Have Heard on High" (Traditional French Melody)

cresc.

f

ff

Away in a Manger

In the setting of Camille Saint-Saens' *Le Cyne*

JAMES R. MURRAY
Arranged by Carolyne M. Taylor

Adagio ♩= ca. 72

Consider these Christmas
writers featured in "All th

CHRISTMAS UNENDING

An anthology of seasonal arrangements and medleys for solo piano from arranger Phillip Keveren. The stand-alone carol settings, with options for creating medleys, make this an ideal resource for banquets requiring dinner music. Titles include *O Come, All Ye Faithful; Angels We Have Heard on High; It Came upon the Midnight Clear; Hark! the Herald Angels Sing; Joy to the World.* Moderate. **MC-525**

YULETIDE TREASURES

Jolene Boyd's collection of Christmas favorites consists of shorter arrangements especially useful for offertories or for "traveling music" in Christmas concerts. Rich harmonies throughout. Titles include: *Angels We Have Heard on High; Away in a Manger; Deck the Halls; God Rest Ye Merry, Gentlemen; It Came upon the Midnight Clear; Jingle Bell Lullaby; Joy to the World; O Christmas Tree; O Little Town of Bethlehem; Silent Night; We Three Kings; While Shepherds Watched Their Flocks.* Moderately easy. **MC-502**

CHRISTMAS REFLECTIONS FOR PIANO

Eleven mellow arrangements of traditional Christmas carols by Teresa Wilhelmi. Uses creative harmonies, fresh yet tasteful treatments. Sample songs: *What Child Is This?; Go, Tell It on the Mountain; We Three Kings; Lully, Lullay, Thou Tiny Child; The Birthday of a King; Good King Wenceslas; Christmas Montage.* Moderate. **MC-264**